Bruce Eric Kaplan

# This Is a Bad Time

*A Collection of Cartoons*

Simon & Schuster

New York   London   Toronto   Sydney

SIMON & SCHUSTER
Rockefeller Center
1230 Avenue of the Americas
New York, NY 10020

Of the 182 cartoons in this collection, 153 originally appeared in *The New Yorker* and were
copyrighted © in 1998, 1999, 2000, 2001, and 2002 by The New Yorker Magazine, Inc. Other cartoons
in this collection originally appeared in *L.A. Weekly, Fast Company,* and *The Boston Globe.*

For information about special discounts for bulk purchases, please contact
Simon & Schuster Special Sales: 1-800-456-6798 or business@simonandschuster.com

Manufactured in the United States of America

1  3  5  7  9  10  8  6  4  2

Library of Congress Cataloging-in-Publication Data

Kaplan, Bruce Eric.
This is a bad time : a collection of cartoons /Bruce Eric Kaplan.
1. American wit and humor, Pictorial. I. Title.
p.   cm.
NC1429.K268A4   2004
741.5'973 22—dc22      2003063311

ISBN 978-1-4516-3641-3

# INTRODUCTION

WHEN I FIRST started drawing cartoons, I lived in a very small apartment in Los Angeles on a shady street near the corner of Fairfax and Willoughby. It was the second floor of a two-car garage. Actually, it was half of the second floor. In the other half lived my neighbor Sharon. Sharon was okay, but her laugh carried. Which was bad, but not as bad as the family who lived in the building about five inches from my window. They generated an ungodly amount of noise, most of it centered around a baby that they seemed to call "cha–tool" for some reason.

So there I was, living in a space that was meant to hold just one car and maybe some old boxes or tools or whatever it is people put in (half of) a garage. I had very few possessions, but, even so, it was quite cramped in there. That's why I drew not at a table but sitting on my bed, hunched over like some kind of beetle. After a few months of that, my back began to hurt from the hunching, and I came up with a new system. I sat on the floor and placed my pad on the low platform bed, atop which a flat, flat futon rested.

Oh God, remember futons? This was the late eighties, and I was in my early twenties. I had come to Los Angeles thinking I would stay for a year or two. But, of course, I never left. I just drifted from one bad assistant job in the entertainment business to another. For many reasons too horrific to go into, the worst was as a production assistant on a cerebral palsy telethon where the entire staff was at war with each other. That was one surreal nightmare . . . and it just went on and on and on.

For a while, I had a steady job as an assistant to a television producer of variety specials, but then he went to Europe for six weeks. He didn't want to pay me while he was away, so he indentured me to a writer friend of his during the interim. Does any of this make any sense? Maybe you had to be in Los Angeles in the late eighties. But, to tell you the truth, I was and it didn't.

Now I was the assistant to this woman who hadn't written anything that had been produced in ten years. And so she had gone mad, although naturally she had been very highly paid in her downward descent. It was unclear why she needed me since the only thing she ever wanted me to do was to pick up two-liter bottles of Diet Sprite for her. She made this request constantly, over and over again. She would call from various locations around the city, asking me to go to the supermarket and drop them off at her undecorated house in the Hollywood hills. I would say, "But, ————, you already have a lot of bottles in the pantry. I put some in there yesterday." She would be annoyed when I pointed this out, but she didn't back down. She needed her Diet Sprite, I needed to support myself, and so the pantry got more and more crowded. She must have drunk some now and then, but, honestly, she didn't even seem to care much for Diet Sprite.

I wish I could say that my personal life was better than my professional life at this time. But it wasn't. I took random stabs at romantic relationships, but somehow I could never seem to . . . now why am I telling you all this? I'm not sure, except that I was just thumbing through the drawings in this collection, and I stopped to look at one and remembered that I was sitting on the floor of the half of the second story of a garage on a street off Fairfax when I drew it. And I remember which job was paying my bills at the time, who I was not in love with, and what song was being played every ten minutes on the radio. I also remember what I was scared of, how intensely I held my beliefs (which, of course, changed moment by moment) and what people in my life intimidated me. The particular drawing that I stopped at was, in fact, inspired by a person who intimidated me back then—it was someone I had gone to college with who was now much more successful than I was (not that that was so hard) and utterly comfortable with himself and confident of his "gifts." I thought, I could never be that comfortable with myself, and wondered why. The result of these ruminations was a cartoon about a contemplative fish who should perhaps be more secure.

Which is all to say that these drawings are really my journals. I use them to explore whatever I find interesting, confusing, or upsetting on any given day. But here's the beauty part—these private thoughts are filtered through the prism of moody children and blasé pets, disillusioned middle-aged men and weary matrons, among others. And so I get to work through whatever I am thinking about in a coded way. No one but me will ever know what the real seed of each image and caption was. So I can be as free as I want to say whatever I want, and no one can catch me. It's great.

Every morning (to this day, I have the same routine, except now I have a desk, albeit a pretty crappy one), I sit down and think about why I am disgruntled or why I am not as disgruntled as I was yesterday and out come these little drawings . . . after much angst and staring into space and occasional lying on the ground moaning. And each week I send off ten or so to *The New Yorker*. And maybe the magazine buys one or two. (Or very often, none. I might mention here, that sometimes I merely pump out insane bile that wouldn't interest one single person on the planet, just like any other journal writer.)

And then, finally, they are published. Mostly in *The New Yorker*, but sometimes in other places as well, such as *L.A. Weekly*. Maybe they appear days after I did them, but sometimes it is weeks, or months, or even years. And when I look at them, I think back to why I drew whatever I drew and I laugh. Or sometimes cringe. Or, every now and then, just wonder what the hell was wrong with me.

You know, now that I have told you all this, I feel slightly embarrassed. But, still, here they are, reader. I open them up to you, and I hope you enjoy them in some way.

*Bruce Eric Kaplan*
*Los Angeles, California*

# This Is a Bad Time

"You'll have to excuse me—I'm myself today."

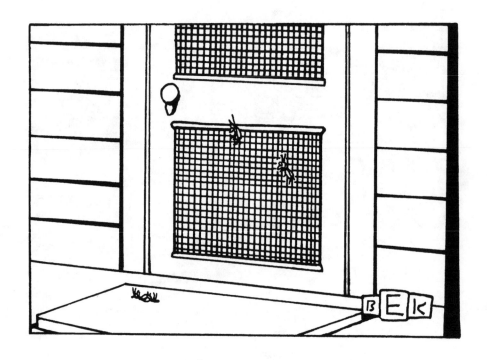

*"He will be greatly missed, both on and off the screen."*

"*I think you'll like this idea—it's sort of dull'*
*meets 'inoffensive.'*"

"He divides his time between here and insanity."

5

"In the future, everyone's going to stop talking about being famous for fifteen minutes."

*"And I don't seem any closer to figuring out why I'm not granting my own wishes."*

8

*"Hey, great death!"*

"We've done a lot of important playing here today."

*"I miss that sense of fulfillment I had when I was part of a plague."*

"I'm warning you—I'm going to call the police if you
don't stop touching base with me."

"*Also included in the package is a vague sense of your not being good enough to stay here.*"

"Sometimes you just option it because your gut tells you this is a book that has to be butchered."

"It's the naps you don't take that you regret the most."

"How do you get your children not to stick to the bottom of the cauldron?"

"I'm scared. Can I sleep with you tonight?"

"*In my day, people died.*"

*"This isn't a hasty decision. A lot of daydreaming*
*went into it."*

"*I like his earlier work, particularly the ones I said
I didn't like at the time.*"

"I don't know why I know all this useless
carrot trivia."

"He did it my way."

*"That's just so God."*

*"Try falling down and scraping your knee. Then you can talk to me about pain."*

25

"*Lately I've been doing the whole dumb expression thing.*"

"No, no, no—stay as late as you want. In fact,
divorce me."

"Every time he comes back from being sheared, we have to spend hours talking about how vulnerable he feels."

"Of course I care about how you imagined I thought
you perceived I wanted you to feel."

"I had a lot of nine-to-five jobs before I realized I
needed to pretend to be creative."

"*Well, as we thought, it's something gross.*"

"*Do that thing where you leave.*"

"*I hear the streets are paved with garbage.*"

"*You always think this is going to be the sconce that changes everything for you.*"

"I'm crazed with this noble path—let me
get back to you."

*"Your priorities change once you get a new toy."*

"You know, Einstein never watched any great
television until after he was forty."

*"We had these twigs flown in from Italy."*

"You do the hokeypokey and you turn yourself
around—that's what it's all about."

"From 3 A.M. to four-thirty, I have you wondering if everything in your life has been a mistake."

*"Sometimes I think he can understand every word we're saying."*

*"She's on her fifth soul mate."*

*"Do you even know how long it's been since
you last poked and prodded me?"*

*"If only I hated then who I hate now."*

"Bad news—we're all out of our minds. You're going to have to be the lone healthy person in this family."

"*I like things to be done my own particular way
by someone other than me.*"

*"We have to believe we're not endangered*
*or we'll all go mad."*

*"Oh, and c.c. the Devil."*

"Sometimes I wonder if there's more to life than
unlocking the mysteries of the universe."

*"Do you want to see where I fester?"*

"I'm sure you two will discover that you're both plagued by a lot of the same nonexistent problems."

*"Did he have any distinguishing characteristics besides
a strong sense of entitlement?"*

"It's easy. The first step is to entirely change
who you are."

*"You stink from the head."*

*"What is this endless series of meaningless experiences trying to teach me?"*

*"I'm the lot of baggage he comes with."*

"You should find solace in the fact that he left behind
such a large body of nuts."

"I don't like all the responsibility that comes
with my new pompousness."

*"I don't believe in egrets."*

*"Somehow, in all the confusion, I aged."*

*"Where do you come up with your rationalizations*
*for not writing?"*

*"I'm still a work-in-hiding."*

*"I want the whole package—the little bowl, the colored pebbles, the plastic castle."*

*"They grow up so slow."*

"*What goes around comes around more annoying.*"

"*I only sniffed his ass to be polite.*"

"What a day! You wouldn't believe the hellacious
archetypes I had to deal with."

"He'd rather be home by himself, staring into space. I can't compete with that."

"I'd read so much about it beforehand that I couldn't help
being disappointed when I actually became enlightened."

*"Where do you see yourself getting drunk*
*in five years?"*

"Not at all. We're just breeding contempt."

"*The first step is to say to yourself, 'Yes, I'm pesky.'*"

"I can see you drew heavily from your
own bad writing."

"*Does my body make me look fat?*"

"I do have a special someone, but he sucks."

"Oh, thanks—I figured that as long as I was having
the thorn taken out of my paw I might as well have a
body scrub and get my mane redone."

"*This is a little embarrassing to admit, but everything that happens happens for no real reason.*"

"It's probably a combination of stress and holding your
basket the wrong way."

*"Doing something never solves anything."*

*"It was a little preachy."*

*"Are you kidding? I'd kill to have your warts."*

"It's amazing what passes for people these days."

"*You know, in some cultures the male does things.*"

*"Monkey see, monkey overanalyze."*

"*The problems will remain the same, but apparently they get wordier and wordier.*"

*"It's completely different for spoiled bitches today."*

*"They don't have the secrets to anything—they're just old."*

"My name is Brett and I'll be the person you focus all
your misplaced anger on for the evening."

*"Oh, by the way, your three-o'clock got squashed."*

"Where are all the new overrated geniuses?"

"*Look, the perception is that you're starving.*"

*"You're only trying to migrate from yourself."*

"He wrote it yesterday and it's still relevant today."

"What did people do before they could read about the
same handful of famous people over and over again?"

"*Now they're saying shiny things attached to hooks are bad for you.*"

"When did we become the bad guys?"

"Maybe I'm never going to find the person I'm supposed to do a real number on."

*"It makes me realize how small you are."*

"*You can wrap it up in a pretty package,*
*but it's still life.*"

"*Look, I'm sorry—I just didn't respond
to the material.*"

"I'm not quite ready yet. Why don't you come in and
make us a drink while I figure out how not to project
all my hopes and fears onto you?"

*"Life sucks and then you keep living."*

*"This little piggy got totally screwed by the market."*

"Hey, I'll do the kvelling around here."

"Sometimes I get so bored with myself I can
barely make it to 'doodle-do.'"

*"You always see the glass as half trying to kill you."*

*"He doesn't understand that I have certain needs I have to talk about all day long."*

*"Here—in case you ever need a shoulder to cry on."*

"*I don't think good huffing and puffing can be taught.*"

"I'm sure it's nothing."

*"It says in lieu of gifts we should not show up."*

"*Just try to get one to answer a riddle* after *he's won your hand in marriage.*"

*"I'm trying to position myself as loyal."*

"*This is perfect. I could stay like this for the*
*next five seconds.*"

*"And our perfunctory sex life is good."*

"Just tell me about the new continent. I don't give a
damn what you've discovered about yourself."

"*Thanks for dinner and the journey to your dark side.*"

"Maybe you could make the hunter more likable."

121

"I don't know if I'm untamed or if I just have a fear
of being ridden."

*"Wait a second—you and I still have a lot of finished business."*

"I'm sorry—here I am going on and on and I haven't
asked you a thing about being caught in a trap."

"Why do you always get to be the gay icon?"

"I just don't want to end up like me."

*"Why would He take someone so toned?"*

"I guess I always knew I wanted to be someone
who puts down writers."

*"I put some things on your desk for you to sign,
misplace, then say you never saw."*

*"I'm in this for the momentary haul."*

"Do you want to be vaguely dissatisfied
with Italian or Korean?"

"*What did I tell you about destroying
Mommy's inner balance?*"

"He's not Asian influenced, he's Asian."

"Sometimes it's important to stop whatever break
you're taking and just do the work."

*"First, I storyboarded it."*

"I'm so tired of the future."

"I just hope inspiration will hit and I'll be
derivative of the right idea."

"Now I look back at that Pied Piper and wonder
why I was so obsessed with him."

"The inflatable pool is a harsh mistress."

"*I do want to solve all my problems, but I'll wait till it comes out in soft cover.*"

"*I recommend an aggressive form of throwing
money at me.*"

"It was another long dark night of the soul patch."

"Why do you automatically assume that I'll fly
too close to the sun?"

*"Okay, so this field is just an illusion—go on."*

"I probably shouldn't do any heavy
shifting of consciousness."

*"Look, the numbers don't lie."*

*"We met cute, but we didn't continue cute."*

*"So you're saying that the message is the cloud itself?"*

*"You can't keep comparing yourself to those skinny*
*little aliens you see in movies."*

"Once you have children, it forever changes the way
you bore other people."

153

"I don't understand how people with full lives do it."

*"O.K., you told me so. May I continue?"*

*"I liked it, except for you."*

"I was reading somewhere that people are stupid."

"This isn't really about water. It's about what's
going on between us."

"He was conceived in a fit of irony."

"I like it—I'm just not sure it's what I
want to rot on."

"*I want to go back to how things were before*
*we knew each other.*"

"He inappropriately touched the lives
of everyone he met."

"*Don't walk away from me while I'm not paying any attention to you.*"

*"It was an incredible journey, but a crappy life."*

"Oh, I was looking for something with
a little more hay."

"*There just aren't any good parts for women over forty who think they can act.*"

"It's so silly. Now I can't even remember
why I killed him."

"To tell you the truth, even when I'm in water I don't feel that comfortable."

"It's very me, but I hate myself."

"*Maybe you should ask yourself why you're inviting all this duck hunting into your life right now.*"

*"So did the fair princess ever develop melanoma?"*

"*I just feel as women we should scratch and bite one another.*"

*"Where's your section of books that tell you simple*
*things you already know?"*

*"If you'll have me, I'd like to be your blind spot."*

*"I realize that each day is a gift. Now it's just a matter of figuring out how to exchange fourteen thousand six hundred of them."*

*"I'd like to believe we're redefining the way future
generations will waste their time."*

*"Sometimes when I look at what goes on, I'm glad I don't really exist."*

*"Is this what I want to be doing with my death?"*